Born Wild

in GLACIER NATIONAL PARK

Photography of **DONALD M. JONES**

ABOVE: A white-tailed ptarmigan chick navigates a small creek high on Logan Pass.

RIGHT: Two bighorn lambs take a break from feeding and playing in a meadow filled with dandelions.

TITLE PAGE: This three-month-old black bear cub makes use of its needle-like teeth on a willow sapling.

FRONT COVER: A wet black bear cub in a rare, and brief, moment of stillness.

BACK COVER: Playful coyote pup; red-necked grebe mother and chick.

ISBN: 978-1-56037-355-1

© 2005 by Farcountry Press
Photography and text © 2005 by Donald M. Jones

For more information on our books, write Farcountry Press, P.O. Box 5630, Helena, MT 59604, call 800-821-3874, or visit www.farcountrypress.com.

Produced in the United States of America.
Printed in China.

20 19 18 17 16   6 7 8 9 10

Dedication

To my mother, who did such a great job in raising her six wild babies. Love you, Mom!

While its mother feeds on spring grasses below, a black bear cub sits patiently in a lodgepole pine.

Spring comes late to much of Glacier National Park, a land where tall peaks and steep slopes are held in winter's frigid grasp for up to 9 months out of the year. Snow and cold may linger, but life manages to emerge from the seemingly inhospitable climes.

This new life returns to Glacier at a time when most of us are still stoking our wood stoves. Great horned owls, red crossbills, and Clark's nutcrackers are busy tending to their nests in March. Grizzly and black bears have given birth but remain snug and warm in their dens until they emerge in April.

With the arrival of April's longer, warmer days, spring migrants start their ritual of returning to the park. By late April and early May, harlequin ducks make their way back from the coast to congregate and pair off along McDonald Creek. Varied thrushes bring song back to the dark cedar forests, and American dippers flutter along rushing creeks in search of water insects to feed their young, which wait in moss-lined nests.

The month of May brings even more warmth; the sun rises higher in the sky with each passing day. Soon, bear cubs are seen scampering behind their mothers, who seem to be in a steady search of nutritious food. Higher up, mountain goat nannies and bighorn ewes are heading to traditional bearing grounds. At lower elevations, the end of May signals the time for cow moose and elk, along with whitetail and mule deer does, to usher in new life.

Though spring is a time of rebirth in Glacier

National Park, the common visitor may not bear witness to that fact. Baby animals are in their most vulnerable state during the first couple of weeks of life. Therefore, a good mother will do what she can to keep harm from coming to her young. This generally comes in the form of concealment, be it hiding her young, camouflaging her young, or becoming more nocturnal in her habits, thus being alert during times of predation. By mid-June, wild animal babies become more conspicuous, and by mid-July it is not uncommon to see Glacier National Park's new creatures, in all their glory, running in the meadows or up the rocky slopes or splashing in one of the park's many lakes.

As you turn the pages of this book, you will see images of many subjects, birds and mammals, all of which were photographed in the wild. All of the photographs were taken from a respectful distance (most were taken with the mother present)—mothers made no abrupt behavioral changes that could be considered aggressively defensive. I photograph from blinds or hides, which allow me to blend in with landscape and cause as little disruption as possible. All of the photographs of bears were taken from the road.

I hope that you enjoy the images that follow and, during your visit to Glacier National Park, find the opportunity to witness some of its junior residents.

Take in all that Glacier National Park has to offer—its trails, its lakes, its vistas, and especially its abundant yet fragile wildlife. Remember that wild is how you found it and wild is how you should leave it. Enjoy!

A mountain goat kid poses innocently on a mountainside.

LEFT: This grizzly cub takes one last look at the tourists lined up along Many Glacier Road before following its mother to higher and safer ground.

BELOW: A mountain goat kid takes a long stretch after a morning nap.

FACING PAGE: As if ready for a game of fetch, a coyote pup chews playfully on a stick.

A moose calf pauses to cast a backward glance while ambling through a dense stand of lodgepole pine.

A black bear cub that has ventured out onto a limb that's too small to carry its bulk finds itself clinging by its tiny teeth. Not to worry: the cub is a mere 3 feet above a bed of soft spring grass.

ABOVE: While perched high in a cotton-wood, a young great horned owl naps in the glow of morning.

RIGHT: A grizzly bear yearling rises up onto its hind legs for a better view.

FACING PAGE: A whitetail doe dutifully cleans the face of one of her two fawns.

An otter family takes a brief break from
fishing on a cold February morning.

LEFT: Bighorn lambs stay close to their mothers during the first winter.

BELOW: A mountain goat nanny leads her kid across a spring snowscape high on Logan Pass.

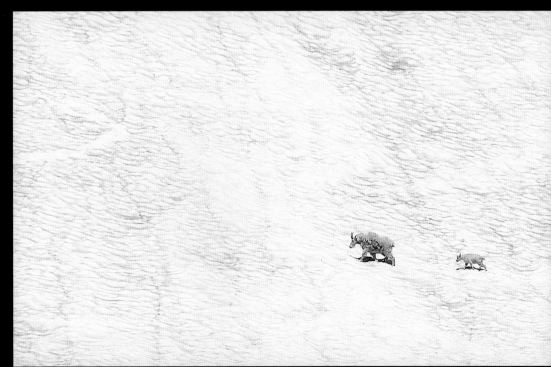

Urged back to the trees by its mother, a black bear cub stands, clutching a small limb, ready to climb to safety at its mother's command.

With Bear Hat Mountain looming in the background, a mountain goat nanny and kid take in the warm sunshine.

RIGHT: This young least chipmunk is dwarfed by a dandelion.

BELOW: A young great horned owl awakes from its nap and stretches its wings. One day its wingspan may reach as much as 4½ feet.

FACING PAGE: You're it! Two fox kits play near their den's entrance.

ABOVE: A three-month-old black bear cub peers at the camera through low vegetation. Born weighing about twelve ounces, they emerge from the den at about ten pounds.

RIGHT: After a cautious backward glance, an elk calf makes its way through a dense stand of spruce to rejoin its mother.

Loons can be found at a number of low-lying lakes around Glacier National Park. Chicks ride on their mothers' backs for safety.

ABOVE: Found throughout Glacier National Park, red-tailed hawks raise between one and four young.

FACING PAGE: A grizzly cub hams it up for the camera from the safety of its mother's side.

ABOVE: With a virtually insatiable appetite, a young black-capped chickadee cries out for more food.

LEFT: A very young coyote pup, just a few weeks old, peeks out from its den.

FACING PAGE: Exhausted from a full day of play, this bighorn lamb takes a nap in the last light of evening.

ABOVE: A young great gray owl, looking a bit perplexed, studies the photographer below. This owlet will grow into one of North America's largest owls, with a wingspan of nearly 5 feet.

RIGHT: A cow elk gives her calf a final brush of her tongue before it ventures off into a nearby opening to romp with the other calves.

FACING PAGE: Perched atop a Douglas fir snag, a black bear cub seems to be saying, "This isn't as comfortable as it looks."

A mother grizzly leads her 2½-year-old cub across a snow-field near Logan Pass in late spring.

ABOVE: A black bear cub grasps the side of a tree, contemplating whether to climb or to run to its mother's side.

LEFT: Two newborn bighorn lambs pause in their game of tag to identify the visitor on their slope.

27

RIGHT: Is this a future center for the Chicago Bears? Probably not—more likely a cub with an insatiable curiosity for everything that's within its grasp.

BELOW: A young pika learns quickly that storing winter's food cache takes precedence over just about everything else. Winters are long in the high country and, unlike squirrels, these little creatures do not hibernate.

This male red-necked grebe offers its young, upon the mother's back, a Thanksgiving-size meal. The male finally gave up on trying to feed the large fish to the small bird and returned with a much more appropriate sampling (a minnow).

ABOVE: This yearling grizzly used its nose like a radar, turning it right then left in an attempt to catch a scent.

RIGHT: This little coyote pup didn't quite know how to react to the noise of the camera coming from what he thought was just a pile of bushes (the photographer's photo blind).

A mountain goat kid stays on the uphill side of its mother for both protection and shade.

This red fox mother, upon returning to the den,
gets no shortage of affection from her brood of kits.

A mistletoe clump in a spruce tree serves as the perfect bed for a snoozing black bear cub.

A whitetail fawn rests in a meadow along the North Fork Road.

RIGHT: A young black-backed three-toed woodpecker peers from its nesting cavity.

BELOW: From the shoreline, the photographer receives an intense stare from a young beaver plying the river.

ABOVE: A coyote pup torments its sibling.

LEFT: This yearling grizzly seems to have had a bad day.

ABOVE: Canada goose and gosling. When threatened, a mother will take on creatures many times her size in order to protect her young.

LEFT: Born to climb, black bear cubs can rival some squirrels in their ability to ascend trees.

A cow moose brings her calf to the lake's edge to feed on lush, green lily pads, which help her to produce the rich milk that her calf needs.

RIGHT: With hummingbirds, such as these calliope babies, either you get along with your siblings or you jump out of the nest prematurely—space is at a premium.

BELOW: As these two black bear cubs (one brown and one black) nursed, it sounded like a combination of kittens purring and birds chirping.

FACING PAGE: Looking more like a kitten, this tiny coyote pup ventures from its den in search of adventure.

These sibling black bear cubs were constantly at play. If they weren't biting sticks, leaves, or rocks, they were biting each other.

With claws like those of this yearling grizzly, satisfying an itch is a snap.

From high on the rocky slopes, a mountain goat nanny and kid survey their surroundings.

Don't worry, this baby porcupine has no problem holding on to this tree limb and will spend a good part of its life doing just that.

RIGHT: Black bear mothers will often place their cubs near a suitable tree, so if danger comes, escape is not far away.

BELOW: A bighorn ewe leads her lamb along steep rock faces in search of food in early winter.

ABOVE: A female northern harrier (marsh hawk) sits on her ground nest while one of her newborn chicks pokes out from under her breast feathers.

RIGHT: Care to dance? Two grizzly cubs at play.

A bighorn lamb
affectionately greets
its mother.

A whitetail fawn steps out into the warm morning light near Camas Road.

LEFT: Four fox kits listen intently at their den entrance as they hear the whir of the motor drive of the photographer's camera.

BELOW: It's rained all morning and this black bear cub vigorously shakes himself dry.

ABOVE: These coyote pups enjoy one another's company at the den site. Playtime is short lived; by summer's end, survival takes priority.

RIGHT: A young Columbian ground squirrel surveys its home area, now covered with glacier lilies, atop Logan Pass.

ABOVE: An American dipper chick squawks from a rock in McDonald Creek while waiting for its mother to deliver a mouth-watering beak full of juicy insects.

RIGHT: A grizzly cub shows off its flexibility, exposing an almost human-like foot.

Coyote pups
wear the marks
of a day of
wrestling
and playing.

RIGHT: A mountain goat nanny and kid walk near the Hidden Lake trail at Logan Pass on a sunny October day.

BELOW: A young hoary marmot suns itself on a rock.

RIGHT: A young red squirrel sits on a bare limb, with golden aspen as a backdrop.

BELOW: A Canada goose gosling lets out a yawn while nestled in the grass with its siblings.

FACING PAGE: This black bear cub obviously hasn't read the "Do Not Pick the Wildflowers" signs in the park.

LEFT: A great gray owl chick stretches its body in order to look like an extension of the tree on which it is perched. The owlet is very vulnerable at this age and camouflage is essential.

BELOW: Like all young creatures, this elk calf is very vulnerable to predators. Calves lie completely flat when danger lurks nearby.

FACING PAGE: A grizzly cub joins its mother for a drink at a near-by spring. Water is fine, but this cub prefers its mother's milk, something she will provide every two or three hours.

A mountain goat kid poses for a portrait. The kid will stay with its mother only for the first year, at which time she will raise another kid.

A black bear cub expresses himself from high up in a spruce tree.

RIGHT: This great gray owlet turned its head completely backward to look at the camera.

BELOW: Two mountain goat kids play "king of the hill" atop a rock.

FACING PAGE: A Columbian ground squirrel warms itself in the spring sunshine.

A black bear cub rolls blissfully in the cool grass.

The effects of a
hard day at play.

LEFT: One day, this coyote pup will use its teeth for more than just chewing on an old log.

BELOW: About fifteen minutes after being sent up a tree by its mother, this black bear cub navigated its way through the branches for a better view.

Although these grizzly cubs have been startled and appear nervous, their mother remains calm and, after a careful look around, continues to feed.

"Hey guys, how about a little help?" Three black bear cubs wrestle and play.

Under the protective guard of its mother, this mountain goat kid rests peacefully.

RIGHT: A young short-eared owl finds the photographer a curious sight.

BELOW: A whitetail fawn ventures to the water's edge on a hot July day. The fawn is now old enough to join its mother on most of her feeding excursions.

Like a lion on a rock throne, this coyote pup looks as if it is the king of the wilderness.

LEFT: From atop a rock, a young golden-mantled ground squirrel looks sheepishly into the camera.

BELOW: A two-week-old bighorn lamb rushes to catch up with its mother.

FACING PAGE: This three-month-old black bear cub strikes a charming pose.

ABOVE: In order to feed on low-growing vegetation buried in the snow, a moose calf must get on its knees.

RIGHT: A two-month-old grizzly cub stands at attention before running to catch up with its mother. Cubs stay with their mothers until the third spring, at which time they go off on their own and the sows breed again.

FACING PAGE: A mountain goat nanny keeps a careful eye on her three-week-old kid. Mountain goats are found throughout Glacier National Park's high country, with Logan Pass being the best spot for viewing—often right in the parking lot of the visitors center.

RIGHT: Young common ravens call from their nest high on a rock cliff. One of Glacier National Park's hardiest residents, ravens are found there year round; on some frigid winter days, they may be the only bird seen.

BELOW: Two mule deer fawns make their way across an open hillside on a hot summer afternoon.

FACING PAGE: A black bear cub stands on its hind legs and plays with a spruce bow. Black bears display a variety of color phases, from black to brown to blond.

Donald M. Jones has spent nearly twenty years photographing wild animals, traveling from the Florida Everglades to the Arctic to the deserts of the Southwest. Don has resided in the small town of Troy, Montana, for the past twenty years with his wife Tess and sons Jake and Luke. This is Don's third book with Farcountry Press, the first two being *Montana Wildlife Portfolio* (2003) and *Rocky Mountain Elk Portfolio* (2004). Don's work is continually featured in publications such as *Ranger Rick, Wild Animal Babies, Your Big Back Yard, Field & Stream, Outdoor Life, Sports Afield,* and *Montana Magazine*, to name just a few.

All of Don's wildlife images are of wild, free-roaming subjects.

www.donaldmjones.com